The Way Ahead
VOICES ON EDUCATION

VOICES ON EDUCATION BECHTEL, MARIE-FRANÇOISE
BERGER, PETER L. DIRECTOR, INSTITUTE FOR THE STUDY OF
THE BOARD OF MANAGING DIRECTORS, DEUTSCHE BANK AG
PUBLICIST, MUNICH BUEB, BERNHARD DIRECTOR, SCHLOSS
ECONOMIC INTEGRATION, INSTITUTE OF EUROPE RUSSIAN
OF OPERATIONS IN SARAJEVO, UNHCR, SENIOR RESEARCH
STUDY OF CONFLICT, UNIVERSITY OF ULSTER AT COLERAINE
BRIDGE, FRÜHWALD, WOLFGANG PRESIDENT, ALEXANDER VON
DIRECTOR, LONDON SCHOOL OF ECONOMICS AND POLITICAL
COMMUNICATIONS MANAGEMENT, ST. GALLEN, GOEL, ASHOK KUMAR
MANAGEMENT, HYDERABAD, GUTZEIT, STEPHAN PROVOST, EUROPEAN
WEIZMANN INSTITUTE OF SCIENCE, REHOVOT, HASKINS, GABRIELLE
SCHOOL, HENSCHEL, THOMAS R. DIRECTOR, EUROPEAN SCHOOL
MARKETING AND DEVELOPMENT, FRANKFURT INTERNATIONAL
UNIVERSITY MARBURG, LEHMANN, MAIK CHAIRMAN, "SCHOOLS
AMBASSADOR TO THE FEDERAL REPUBLIC OF GERMANY, MEMBER
CHRISTIAN PRESIDENT, GERMAN ACADEMY OF LANGUAGE AND
STATION ST. PETER, COLOGNE, MÜLLER, HARALD MANAGING

DIRECTEUR, ECOLE NATIONALE D'ADMINISTRATION (ENA), PARIS, ECONOMIC CULTURE, BOSTON, BREUER, ROLF-E. SPOKESMAN OF FRANKFURT/MAIN, BRINCK, CHRISTINE JOURNALIST AND SALEM SCHOOL, BUTORINA, OLGA HEAD OF SECTOR, EUROPEAN ACADEMY OF SCIENCE, MOSCOW CUTTS, MARK FORMER CHIEF OFFICER, GENEVA, DUNN, SEAMUS DIRECTOR, CENTRE FOR THE FORSYTH, JOHN CENTRE OF INTERNATIONAL STUDIES, CAM- HUMBOLDT FOUNDATION, BONN, GIDDENS, ANTHONY SCIENCE, GLOTZ, PETER DIRECTOR, INSTITUTE FOR MEDIA AND DIRECTOR, NATIONAL INSTITUTE OF AGRICULTURAL EXTENSION COLLEGE OF LIBERAL ARTS, BERLIN, HARARI, HAIM PRESIDENT, THE DIRECTOR, SENIOR EXECUTIVE PROGRAMME, LONDON BUSINESS OF GOVERNANCE, BERLIN, HODGSON, ADELE DIRECTOR SCHOOL, KAESLER, DIRK PROFESSOR OF SOCIOLOGY, PHILIPPS- ONLINE", MALLABY, SIR CHRISTOPHER FORMER BRITISH OF THE BOARD OF TRUSTEES, TATE GALLERY LONDON, MEIER, LITERATURE, MENNEKES S.J., FRIEDHELM DIRECTOR, KUNST- DIRECTOR, PEACE RESEARCH INSTITUTE, FRANKFURT/MAIN,

MÜLLER-MAGUHN, ANDY SPOKESMAN, CHAOS COMPUTER CLUB
MURRAY & ASSOCIATES, HONG KONG, NEUBERGER, JULIA CHIEF
DIRECTOR, FEDERAL CHANCELLERY, BERLIN, ÖZDEMIR, CEM MP
BERLIN, PLESU, ANDREI RECTOR OF THE NEW EUROPE COLLEGE
OF FOREIGN AFFAIRS, BUCHAREST, PRIMOR, AVI FORMER ISRAELI
PRESIDENT OF TEL AVIV UNIVERSITY, PULZER, PETER GLADSTONE
TRATION, ALL SOULS COLLEGE, OXFORD, PUTTNAM, LORD DAVID
JOACHIM DIRECTOR EMERITUS, MAX-PLANCK-INSTITUTE FOR
PRESIDENT OF THE FEDERAL REPUBLIC OF GERMANY, REINICKE
AND MANAGING DIRECTOR GALAXAR S.A., GENEVA, SCHÖFTHALER
SION, BERLIN, SCHULLER, PHILIPP MEMBER OF THE BOARD
EUROPEAN-UNIVERSITY-VIADRINA, FRANKFURT/ODER, SIMO, DAVID
LITERATURES AND CIVILISATIONS, UNIVERSITY OF YAOUNDÉ
DEFAMATION LEAGUE, NEW YORK, STOLPE, MANFRED PRIME
UNITED NATIONS UNDER-SECRETARY-GENERAL AND RECTOR OF
GRETHE MINISTER OF EDUCATION, DENMARK, WEBER, MONIKA
AND SPORT, ZURICH, WEILER, HANS PROFESSOR EMERITUS OF
WINNACKER, ERNST-LUDWIG PRESIDENT, DEUTSCHE FOR-
PRIMATE, BENEDICTINE ORDER, ROME

HAMBURG, **MURRAY, SIMON** FOUNDER AND CHAIRMAN, SIMON EXECUTIVE, KING'S FUND, LONDON, **NOWAK, WOLFGANG** ASSISTANT SPOKESMAN ON INTERNAL AFFAIRS OF BÜNDNIS 90/DIE GRÜNEN, FORMER ROMANIAN MINISTER OF CULTURE AND MINISTER AMBASSADOR TO THE FEDERAL REPUBLIC OF GERMANY, VICE-PROFESSOR EMERITUS OF GOVERNMENT AND PUBLIC ADMINIS-CHAIRMAN, ENIGMA PRODUCTIONS, LONDON, **QUEISSER, HANS-**SOLID STATE RESEARCH, STUTTGART/GRENOBLE, **RAU, JOHANNES WOLFGANG H.** DIRECTOR, GLOBAL PUBLIC POLICY PROJECT UNO **TRAUGOTT** SECRETARY GENERAL, GERMAN UNESCO COMMIS-DEUTSCHLAND DENKEN! E.V., **SCHWAN, GESINE** PRESIDENT, HEAD OF DEPARTMENT, INSTITUTE FOR MODERN LANGUAGES, **STERN-LAROSA, CARYL** DIRECTOR, EDUCATION DIVISION, ANTI-MINISTER, STATE OF BRANDENBURG, **VAN GINKEL, HANS J.A.** THE UNITED NATIONS UNIVERSITY, TOKYO, **VESTAGER, MAR-**CITY COUNCILLOR, HEAD OF THE DEPARTMENT OF SCHOOLS EDUCATION AND POLITICAL SCIENCE, STANFORD UNIVERSITY, SCHUNGSGEMEINSCHAFT, BONN, **WOLF O.S.B., NOTKER** ABBOT

THE WAY AHEAD: VOICES ON EDUCATION
Susan Stern

2001: This year, the Alfred Herrhausen Society for International Dialogue truly lived up to its name. More than 250 scholars, educators, administrators, politicians and members of the press – representing 24 countries – attended its annual mid-June colloquium in Berlin, making it a truly international event. And there was plenty of opportunity for dialogue as well. In addition to the plenary discussions and lectures that had structured the event in previous years, participants were offered a choice of smaller discussion sessions on specific issues, allowing them to interact with experts and opinion leaders in the field. This year's conference theme, The Way Ahead – Education and the Cutting Edge, certainly warranted the scope of the event and the thoughtfulness that went into putting it together.

FORUM International August/September 2001

When you convoke a gathering of the super-literate, hand-picked from among the intellectual, spiritual and political leaders of Europe and beyond, captains of industry, men and occasionally women who run universities, research institutions and think tanks, representatives of international organisations, outstanding scholars young

and old(er)... well, you can expect something exciting to emerge from it. Especially when the discussion topic is education, which just has to be one of the favourite global flavours of the fledgling new millennium. So when the Alfred Herrhausen Society for International Dialogue (AHG), Deutsche Bank's socio-political forum, put on a star-studded (in the above sense) event to explore the most pressing and controversial issues in the field, it was a good bet that at the very least it would deliver stimulating, provocative talk. And with any luck, talk with the potential to lead to constructive action, because if there was one point on which the 55 active participants and the 250 invited guests appeared to agree from the start, it was that THINGS HAVE TO BE DONE URGENTLY to provide new impetus to education across the globe. Education, everybody agreed, is the world's most important capital, and education across the board is in dire need of rethinking and revamping.

WHAT ARE WE TALKING ABOUT?

What exactly do we mean by education? Peter Berger had a few thoughts on the subject. 'The present conference was conceived in German, but is being executed in English. The key term used to describe the topic of the conference is, in German, Bildung. The term has a venerable history in the German-speaking world at least as far back as the literary genre of the Bildungsroman, and its meaning is considerably broader than that of the English term "education". Literally, it means "formation" – the deliberate design of a certain type of human individual. By contrast, in contemporary English usage "education" (whatever its original Latin meaning) generally refers to formal schooling.' Simon Murray, the Englishman who left school, dashed off to sea and then joined the Foreign Legion before getting into the business of running industrial empires, had his own thoughts on what the educated man might be, and these thoughts were definitely along the *Bildung* lines. 'Given my lack of formal education …I feel a bit at a loss as to what I should say (here today), and I feel a bit like Edward II, King of England in the 13th century, must have felt when he came down to his throne room one morning to find himself confronted with a whole bunch of Frenchmen, and he had no idea why they were there or what he should say to them. So he impro-

vised: "Gentlemen, if the love that I have for you were equal to the lack of knowledge I have on the subject about which you have come to see me, it would know no bounds." Well, he certainly had good communication skills and that was not a bad opening for a man who had never spent a single day in school in his life. He was later described by those French visitors as a man of culture, a man of good taste, a cultivated man – my mother would have said a well brought-up young man. Educated.'

In retrospect, that the bankruptcy of education was a more or less assumed underlying premise at the colloquium was perhaps surprising. Many of us who live in Germany are so accustomed to complaining about the appalling state of our universities, the encrusted structures, the lack of funds, outdated and irrelevant curricula, overcrowded classrooms, tired and ageing faculty, unmotivated and ageing students (and so on) that we are perhaps more likely to take for granted that other countries have much the same woes. In fact, most of them have very different problems with (or, more aptly, without) education. But nowhere, it seems, is education doing what it could and should be doing – whatever that may be.

The value of education

The value put on education these days seems alarmingly low. We are running the risk of failing to understand the importance of education! Only an educated society can find the strength to be innovative and integrated at the same time. Only a society which recognises education as a value can be successful in the long run, can guarantee human dignity and quality of life. ▶ complete on CD

Rolf-E. Breuer

Actually, given the squabble-propensity of academics, who, needless to say, were well represented at the gathering, there was remarkable basic consensus among all present throughout the two days we were together. Education as we now know and practice it in variations on a theme is facing huge challenges in an interconnected world in which the speed of change has accelerated in such a way as to make much of our reform-thinking redundant even before we have formulated it, let alone implemented it. Our world is one of turbo change, although that particular expression was not one which kept recurring as did quite a few others. Globalisation. Cosmopolitanism. Elites-oops-leadership building. Social responsibility (which always followed fast on the heels of elites-oops-leadership building). Innovation. Life-long learning. Knowledge society. Information society. The speakers freely used the terms, well aware that each one was potentially loaded. For apart from the fact that the speakers were all highly educated – with Simon Murray the one notable, self-proclaimed exception – they were not homogeneous, they didn't all come from the same place, either figuratively or literally. And, as we learned, concepts such as globalisation, life-long learning and all the rest have quite different meanings in such far-flung societies as rural India and urban Britain, in emerging and advanced economies. Patent formulae for 'improving education' (usually with

the West telling the emerging economies how to do things, as Gabrielle Haskins noted) simply don't exist.

Well, we probably knew all that before we went to Berlin. In fact, we probably already 'knew' most of what we heard – and to a great extent, that was exactly the point. Because much of what we talked about had a lot less to do with the acquisition of information per se, but rather, with what we make of acquired information, so freely available these days to the more fortunate members of the world population, and how we turn it into useful knowledge. And that was one of the topics we talked a lot about in the end: education as a means to enable people to digest and process the huge quantities of information they are constantly bombarded with and to transform it all into something other than meaningless white noise.

What the conference did was make us probe some sensitive areas – and we all had them. One of the main and recurring discussion areas concerned educational elites – a touchy subject for most educational egalitarians and a particularly touchy issue in the host country Germany, where all education, including professional training and higher education, is considered a basic right for everyone with minimum qualifications (a school leaving certificate), to be paid for by the state. Elite education, the training of future or 'young' leaders, the very recognition that the more talented among us should perhaps be singled

It has been calculated that a daily edition of the "New York Times" contains more information than a 17th century Englishman received in his whole life. This indicates how important judgement and orientation abilities have become. There are many who already feel threatened by this information flood, and complain that the volume of junk data and intensity of information smog are increasing by the day. ▶complete on CD

Johannes Rau

Information smog

University Reform

Anthony Giddens stated it very clearly when he talked about the competition between the London School of Economics, Harvard, MIT, Princeton and other universities:
If Germany is not willing to reform its university system, then it will no longer be able to compete with the big boys abroad. I have no doubt about that...

Peter Glotz

out for special educational treatment (I use the words deliberately) – these notions are anathema to many. And yet, everybody including the German participants seemed to agree that in our 'global' world, in our increasingly interdependent and complex world, effective leaders are needed more than ever and these leaders should be specially trained.

How can a society reconcile the formation of elites with notions of egalitarianism? There were many suggestions. Interestingly enough from a personal perspective, although I had the feeling that the 'Anglo-Saxon model' was generally decried, and not just by the French representative of elite education, I also got the impression that the kind of elite training which was being most touted was in fact the kind being practiced most widely in Anglo-Saxon countries... just with a bit more social responsibility. This meant that 'any large industrial or economic institution has the social responsibility to deal with educational insti-

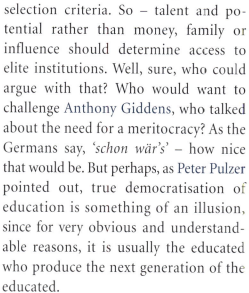

tutions' (Haim Harari). It also meant that far more of the world should be provided access to these institutions, since education in general and elite education in particular are still available to only a very small segment of humanity. And even within that small segment, access to the very best (to the institutions that produce future leadership around the globe) is determined by questionable selection criteria. So – talent and potential rather than money, family or influence should determine access to elite institutions. Well, sure, who could argue with that? Who would want to challenge Anthony Giddens, who talked about the need for a meritocracy? As the Germans say, *'schon wär's'* – how nice that would be. But perhaps, as Peter Pulzer pointed out, true democratisation of education is something of an illusion, since for very obvious and understandable reasons, it is usually the educated who produce the next generation of the educated.

Indeed, education, traditionally considered as a great equaliser, can also be a great divider, and the more specialised knowledge becomes (and as far as I know, nobody questioned this trend),

Inequalities

It is generally accepted that education provides the means to overcome inequalities... Certainly, education can play a major role in countering inequalities. But it is vital to recognize that education also generates inequalities in our contemporary society .... partly because of the transition to the knowledge economy and partly because of the impact of the globalisation of economic activity ... Now, a primary source of inequality lies in skills and the lack thereof at the higher end of society. What we are witnessing worldwide is a new gap separating about 20 percent of the population from the rest because of the specialised skills – computer skills, whatever - that this 20 percent possesses. Since these specialists are scarce and therefore valued by corporations and other employers, their wages are increasing rapidly. But a large percentage of the rest of the workforce are being left behind. So now we have two new sources of inequality, and rather than simply being the means to resolving the problem, education is actually a cause. ▶ complete on CD

Anthony Giddens

Brain Races

What has happened is that there has been a change in the evaluation of the power of states, from one I would call hard power, that is to say the possession of the instruments of destruction... towards soft power, the power of economies, the power of innovation, the power of educational and cultural influence. And it is that, not the continuing possession of the instruments of destruction, that gives the United States its hegemonial position today. Its soft power lies in the strength of its economy and its currency, in the location there of many of the world's most influential multinational corporations, in the influence that its highest and best educational institutions have in both teaching and research... What has happened and what has, I hope, been finally confirmed by the end of the Cold War, is the substitution of brain races for arms races. The terms of competition are now not armies or navies or air forces, nor military technology, but achievement. And not only achievement, but reputation. ▶ complete on CD

Peter Pulzer

the greater the gap between the knowledge 'haves' and the knowledge 'have-nots'. This was a theme which ran through the entire colloquium. Whereas in the 'old' days, education helped smooth out inequalities at the bottom rungs of society, it now creates inequalities at the top. And even among the knowledge 'haves', there is a frightening lack of internal communication, simply because the fields of specialisation are so sophisticated.

Knowledge societies – we live in a software world, one in which our brain power counts more than our weapons. The countries with the best schools, the best research facilities, the best opportunities for lifelong learning – these are the countries with a competitive advantage. And there is a knock-on effect – the better the educational and research facilities of a country, the greater the quality of the people they will attract, the better the facilities will become ... and brain-power will become concentrated in a few locations.

University reform was inevitably on the agenda. Indeed, how could it not be in Germany, where it is generally recognised as being desperately needed and is therefore always on the agenda – to little avail, however, as the country has been in a state of education-reform inertia ever since the post-1968 burst of reform activity. But the ongoing debates evade the crucial issues, charged Stephan Gutzeit. 'We shouldn't think that calling a rose by any other name will change the rose. In Germany, we are talking about changing the name of our degrees. Is it not much more important to talk about content, to talk about what universities should be doing in terms of education? Should they focus on pure science or pure scholarship? Is character education, character building, a legitimate task of universities? How should we design our curricula? How much focus should there be on the acquisition of facts versus the practice of methods? These, I think, are much, much more important and they are very rarely discussed.' In Gutzeit's opinion, Germany needs an innovative avant-garde to get ahead.

He was obviously voicing concerns of a community that spreads far beyond Germany and its neighbours. 'While the focus (of the colloquium) was largely on regional issues, at the end of the day, the questions raised were as important for the citizens of Mali as they were for German society.' (Adama Óuane) Given the cosmopolitan aspect of our gathering, it was not surprising that we talked about what a global family we – we the privileged, of course – were, united not so much by fast food à la McDonalds but by communication possibilities, fast travel à la Lufthansa and, of course, by information technology. United by the sheer geographical mobility of our educators as well as of our educatees; for indeed, the academics who once inhabited ivory towers have long since joined the jet-setters and are constantly on the go (albeit often David-Lodge style, from one academic institution to another in different parts of the world). Are we in any danger of seeing this mobility trend reversed through stay-at-home technology? Nobody seriously questioned whether near-future generations of students might be tempted to partake of their educational manna exclusively via the internet and distance learning – having a physical campus, a place to rub shoulders apparently remains a need on the part of most young people, as Anthony Giddens pointed out.

United too, for better or worse, by language: We talked about the need for a common language to make communication between peoples possible, and the all-pervasiveness of English as our lingua franca, a fact accepted by most, regretted by a few, and denounced by one, Marie-Françoise Bechtel, who feared that English was destroying communication between English-speaking elites and their own countrypeople. Other participants too seemed to feel that we were favouring English at the expense of our native tongues, and thus at the expense of our native cultures – they stressed the need for everyone today to be bi- if not polylingual. Quite simply, said Notker Wolf, language is the sine qua non for mutual understanding and is therefore a precondition for peace. However, having established that, we need to distinguish between a conversation or communication language, and the language each of us has to express our own culture.

We talked about communalities, but we talked too about differences – differences in mind-sets, differences in our educational 'points de départ' so to speak. The countries of eastern Europe start out with a number of disadvantages, not the least being that they are not yet very comfortable with English as the de facto lingua franca; their educational institutions lack 'critical mass' and they find it hard(er) to attract foreign students because the creature comforts they have to offer are not up to western standards, and 'such soft factors count' (Gesine Schwan). In stark contrast, other countries have other problems which make ours in the wealthy parts of the globe almost trivial: in some parts of Africa, for example, education means survival and the problems which education has to confront there are far more complex than in the developed world. Here, democratisation of education means making the masses literate, 'a precondition for enabling them to participate in local and global democratic processes, and providing them access to information and markets through the new media' (David Simo). India has its own serious literacy problems: however, in a most impassioned speech, Ashok Kumar Goel explained how a no-cost or low-cost Internet revolution – the marriage of cyber technology with rural oral tradition – could produce an

Lifelong learning is not only opening doors and opportunities but also breaking down walls. It is not only endless learning but also unlearning and forgetting a great deal.

Adama Óuane

Learning

Education

So how much knowledge can a man bear, how much knowledge does he need, how much can he process? In principle, Theodor Fontane answered this question at the end of the 19th century. He is one of the sharpest, perfectly modern critics of a middle-class, ideologically motivated education process, of knowledge ladders that are entirely superfluous except to someone who wants to become a professional quiz-show participant. He wrote to his daughter Methe on August 9th, 1895: "I was almost ready to say: 'education is a world-class catastrophe'. A man must be clever rather than educated. But since education, like a sore throat brought on by a cold eastern wind, can be hardly avoided, we have to be constantly on guard to stop a minor affection from becoming an all-consuming affliction." ▶ complete on CD

Wolfgang Frühwald

almost completely literate Indian subcontinent within the next five to ten years. And again, in another contrast, Margrethe Vestager deplored the illiteracy which is so alarmingly prevalent in the so-called developed nations of the world. 'People do not read and are therefore excluded from the democratic process,' she lamented, although she was talking about a different kind of illiteracy, the inability to read more than cartoons and the tabloids. All in all, the speakers took us from one specific situation to another as we sped around the world and alighted on regional educational needs and deficiencies.

Most of the colloquium speakers focused on higher education, but some were specifically concerned about the teaching of children – and interestingly enough, given all of the possible issues in primary and secondary education that they could have chosen to talk about, almost all discussed some aspect of the need to imbue children with a notion of tolerance. We are still taught national prejudice at school, said Avi Primor, we are taught self-righteousness, we are taught one-sided, biased history. So we desperately need new teaching materials, new history books which present a supra-national perspective. Caryl Stern-LaRosa made a strong case for anti-bias education for all school teachers, since 'We believe very strongly that no-one is born bigoted, that we do not enter the world as little haters but that we learn to hate. And if we learn to hate, we can unlearn to hate.' Peter Berger's talk was not specifically about child education, but he too had something to say on the subject: 'There can be no identity without boundaries. We know from developmental psychology that the child learns who he is through learning who he is not ...There is no necessary antagonism implied by these boundaries. To understand oneself as a child need not imply hostility to adults, little boys do not have to hate little girls, and it is not necessary for a group of A's to be antagonistic to non-A's.' But, he agreed, some boundaries do indeed come to divide friends and enemies. In his talk about the urgent need to provide ongoing education to refugee children, Marc Cutts made the chilling point that if this is not made into a top priority by the so-called 'civilised' countries, then others will rush in to fill the gap. 'Today, many of the Taliban authorities who control Afghanistan were the refugees who attended the ultra-conservative Islamic religious schools in Pakistan. Some would argue that if more had been done to provide alternative and more liberal education, the Taliban movement might not have taken root in the way that it did.'

What indeed should young people be learning in this brave new world of ours? 'The most important area of education innovation has to be enabling people to become full citizens – not only of their own countries or regions, but globally. That means enabling them to use information to make critical decisions' (Julia Neuberger). However, as vital as it is for them to learn how to process facts and information, there are other crucial aspects to education. The forming of character, for example. President Rau talked eloquently about the necessity for educators to provide learners with what he called 'an inner compass' to navigate the ocean of knowledge. 'This inner compass has a lot to do with upbringing. Upbringing starts in the family but it does not stop there. Schools and universities are places where young people are moulded, formed. We need the resolution to provide young people with an education which promotes a sense of self-responsibility and solidarity, as well as responsibility for others.' Just how this educational foundation can best be laid – and what it should consist of – was debated during various discussions, although there were considerably more questions raised than answers suggested. Should the foundation come primarily from the humanities, or should it include the natural sciences? As Ernst-Ludwig Winnacker pointed out when he was summarizing the forum on innovation, there are those in Germany who (still) believe that while it does no harm to know something about the natural sciences, they do not belong on the education agenda. But what, in fact does? And which long-established values should be preserved and drawn upon? Of course young people should be given access to the internet, and a number of speakers talked about how many school children were now 'hooked up' and computer-literate – a huge number in Germany, which until just a few years ago was still at the manual typewriter stage, but a pitiful few in much of the rest of the world. Echoing Anthony Giddens and his keynote speech at the start of the colloquium, many felt that the access to information technology, to cyber-knowledge, is actually exacerbating the divide. Those who are already on the net are well able to make themselves visible, whereas all the rest tend to be drowned out. Wisdom and education cannot be confined to those 20 percent who have access to telephones, radio and the internet; the other 80 percent of the world population must be integrated into the education system.

I cannot emphasise enough that today's society is a knowledge-based society, but within this knowledge, the main economic commodity is not just knowledge, but scientific and technological knowledge. This does not mean that everybody has to be a scientist, an engineer or a technician. But it certainly means that a conversance with scientific and technological issues is already part of a good general education today, and will be more so in the future. Every leader today, every major politician, every government minister, spends a huge percentage of his/her time concerned with issues of science and technology, be it in the field of health or agriculture or the environment or energy or transportation or defence or industry or communications .... And therefore, part of the training of tomorrow's elite has to be multidisciplinary and include science and technology, because tomorrow we will need totally new professions which did not exist yesterday. And education will have to be multidisciplinary from kindergarten to the PhD, and I am not exaggerating at either end.

▶ complete on CD

Haim Harari

Multidisciplinarity

EDUCATION AS A CAPITAL INVESTMENT

'I wish that all banks would get the message and hold seminars such as this – where the capital of today talks about the knowledge of tomorrow,' commented Ashok Kumar Goel, and continued, 'We're used to banks talking about money. For a bank to talk about education is positively futuristic.' Certainly, he was not alone in feeling that Deutsche Bank was making a very important statement about priorities in the modern world – indeed, was making a commitment to what it saw as a top priority: education. Several speakers, starting with keynote speaker Anthony Giddens, referred to Deutsche Bank-supported educational projects. David Puttnam added his gratitude. 'It is corporations such as Deutsche Bank that will tilt the balance in favour of education and against catastrophe.' And from Gabriele Becker, 'Deutsche Bank is pre-destined to play a major role in sponsoring the global dialogue on education'. Education as 'capital' and education as an 'investment' – these themes kept recurring. 'In a post-industrial world, education is our principal capital,' said Viviane Senna. 'An investment in education is the most important investment in the life of any individual,' is the way Stephan Gutzeit put it. And according to Jürgen Kluge, 'knowledge is the capital of the coming era, it yields more than 100 percent interest. Investing in education pays off in spades, especially for industry. A common education initiative is an imperative.' But perhaps the most provocative statement was made by Philipp Schuller. 'I am a banker,' he stated. 'I look at education from the point of view of money spent and money earned. Is education an investment? Does it bring a financial return? Because if it doesn't, it isn't an investment. I am not talking about non-financial returns – education may create a better society, better human beings, but that is not my point here. Education is only an investment if it results in higher incomes in the future. And in fact, this is why most people go to university – a university education allows them to earn higher salaries and lowers their risk of being unemployed.'

The way ahead, that's what it came down to. The colloquium was about education, specifically about the future of education, for what is the point of simply bemoaning the present? We have to bring about positive, innovative change, and this can only be realised if the academic and corporate worlds join forces. 'In this battle (to improve the quality of education), the state can hold the line, but the battle can only be won by the enthusiastic and generous involvement of the private sector,' as David Puttnam expressed it.

Repute

In the registration of patents within the European Union, for which there are reliable statistics, the German per capita contribution is very high; it is, I believe, the second highest in the EU. But where do these registrations come from? The biggest single register of patents in Germany is the firm of Siemens. Now, that is great news for the repute of German industry. It is less good news for the repute of German universities, because if we continue to believe that the unity of research and teaching is a necessity for the maintenance of quality in higher education, we have to note a deficit here. And if we agree that repute acts as a magnet, that the best academics want to teach at the institutions with the highest repute, that the best students want to learn at the institutions with the highest repute, i.e. those with the best research record, then this kind of thing does matter. ▶ complete on CD

Peter Pulzer

At the same time, we have to make sure that industry does not co-opt education for its own (selfish) purposes - 'we have to make sure that companies don't turn classrooms into a market place for their specific products – that classrooms don't become places of edutainment' in the words of Andy Müller-Maguhn. The balance is a delicate one. Industry can, in fact, fill an education void to the detriment of academic institutions.

There are no easy answers. 'It's very difficult to bridge the gap between the academic and corporate worlds,' said Philipp Schuller, 'but that's exactly why we need to talk. We don't need a conference on issues that everyone agrees on.' And yet, as I started out by saying, there appeared to be almost unanimous agreement on the essentials, the overall goals of education in a more perfect world. Judging by their comments during and following the event, most of the participants would agree with Gary Hattem's summation: 'The colloquium tackled the difficult issue of education with great agility. There was little doubt among those who attended that our survival as a civilised world depends on education and enlightenment.' And finally, I think everyone would add their amen to the comment by Hans-Dieter Holtzmann: 'I can only hope that each one of us at this colloquium will return home and direct our resources at transforming what we have learned here into concrete action. We all have a vested interest in our education system.'

GLOBAL REACH AACHEN, ATLANTA, AUGSBURG, BAD HOM

CAMBRIDGE, CHAPEL HILL, COLERAINE, COLOGNE, COPENHAGEN

FIESOLE, FRANKFURT/ MAIN, FRANKFURT/ODER, GENEVA, GÜTERS

KONG, HYDERABAD, JERUSALEM, KARLSRUHE, KASSEL, KOBLENZ

MAINZ, MARBURG, MINSK, MOSCOW, MÜLHEIM/RUHR, MUNICH

PRAGUE, REHOVOT, ROME, SAARBRÜCKEN, SALEM, SANTIAGO DE

TOKYO, TÜBINGEN, TUTZING, VIENNA, WARSAW, WEIMAR, WIES

ATLANTA, AUGSBURG, BAD HOMBURG, BERLIN, BONN, BOSTON

COLERAINE, COLOGNE, COPENHAGEN, DARMSTADT, DRESDEN

MAIN, FRANKFURT/ODER, GENEVA, GÜTERSLOH, HALLE, HAM

JERUSALEM, KARLSRUHE, KASSEL, KOBLENZ, LANCASTER, LEICESTER

MINSK, MOSCOW, MÜLHEIM/RUHR, MUNICH, MÜNSTER, NEW

VOT, ROME, SAARBRÜCKEN, SALEM, SANTIAGO DE CHILE, SAC

TÜBINGEN, TUTZING, VIENNA, WARSAW, WEIMAR, WIESBADEN

BURG, BERLIN, BONN, BOSTON, BRUGGE, BRUSSELS, BUCHAREST,

DARMSTADT, DRESDEN, DÜSSELDORF, ENSCHEDE, ERFURT, ESSEN,

LOH, HALLE, HAMBURG, HEIDELBERG, HOHENKIRCHEN, HONG

LANCASTER, LEICESTERSHIRE, LEIPZIG, LONDON, LUDWIGSHAFEN,

MÜNSTER, NEW YORK, OBBENOVAC, OXFORD, PARIS, POTSDAM,

CHILE, SAO PAULO, ST. GALLEN, STANFORD, STUTTGART, TEL AVIV,

BADEN, WITTENBERG, WÜRZBURG, YAOUNDÉ, ZURICH, AACHEN,

BRUGGE, BRUSSELS, BUCHAREST, CAMBRIDGE, CHAPEL HILL,

DÜSSELDORF, ENSCHEDE, ERFURT, ESSEN, FIESOLE, FRANKFURT/

BURG, HEIDELBERG, HOHENKIRCHEN, HONG KONG, HYDERABAD,

SHIRE, LEIPZIG, LONDON, LUDWIGSHAFEN, MAINZ, MARBURG,

YORK, OBBENOVAC, OXFORD, PARIS, POTSDAM, PRAGUE, REHO-

PAULO, ST. GALLEN, STANFORD, STUTTGART, TEL AVIV, TOKYO,

WITTENBERG, WÜRZBURG, YAOUNDÉ, ZURICH, AACHEN, ATLANTA,

The Gallery

The top-level conference on education ... shows how important the topic is to the corporate world. Whether national economies will succeed or fail depends on how they deal with this "most important issue for the future of the world future", says AHG's advisory board chairman Rolf-E. Breuer.

Frankfurter Rundschau, June 15, 2001

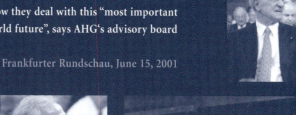

"The current debate on education and knowledge fails to deal sufficiently with the topical issues," said President Rau to top-level representatives of business and academia. Germany needs to muster enough courage to implement an education system that promotes responsibility and solidarity.

Süddeutsche Zeitung, June 16, 2001

Anthony Giddens, Director of the London School of Economics, listed the three key challenges faced by mankind. All of them have to do with education: globalisation, technological change and accelerating customisation... Future elites will be increasingly cosmopolitan in character. That is why education and upbringing will gain in importance.

Der Tagesspiegel, June 16, 2001

"The young generation of managers needs much better training in new technologies." Hans Weiler, professor of Education and Political Studies at Stanford University and one of the panel speakers in Forum 4, says much still needs to be done to properly train and educate the elites.

Frankfurter Allgemeine Zeitung, June 23, 2001

Orientierung für die Zukunft.
Bildung im Wettbewerb.

Alfred Herrhausen Gesellschaft

für internationalen Dialog

EIN FORUM DER DEUTSCHEN BANK

Breuer ... criticised the German system of education for inadequately reflecting Germany's de-facto status as an immigration country. While Berlin's Turkish population is the third-largest in the world, its school system practically ignores this fact.

Berliner Zeitung, June 16, 2001

The Alfred Herrhausen Society's 9th Annual Colloquium brought to Berlin decision makers on educational issues from Germany and many other countries. Apart from the AHG, only the Bertelsmann Foundation and the German government are currently able to put together such a high-level conference.

Das Handelsblatt, July 6-7, 2001

"So many people are still illiterate in India that we have to caution: education should not become a kind of Monopoly game, played by those who have all the opportunities and those who have none", says Kumar Goel, Director of the National Institute of Agriculture in Hyderabad.

Der Tagesspiegel, June 17, 2001

The keynote theme remained unchanged throughout the conference: education is the only kind of investment that can help us cope with the future. Increased competition between countries is already affecting international relations. Germany is aware of this but it hasn't found the courage to do what it takes to improve its rotten education system.

Die Welt, June 19, 2001

Market-oriented reforms: at the 9th Annual Colloquium of the Alfred Herrhausen Society for International Dialogue, business lobbyists energetically demand new directions in educational policy-making.

Frankfurter Rundschau, June 1, 2001

A spectacular show followed by dinner in the Pergamon Museum. "At a very special education summit, the new Berlin shows that it can match New York."

"Da steh ich nun ich armer Thor! Und bin so klug als wie zuvor…"
Johann Wolfgang von Goethe, Faust, Der Tragödie erster Teil

Members of the Board of Trustees

Dr. Rolf-E. Breuer (Chairman), Frankfurt am Main
Dr. Hans D. Barbier, Frankfurt am Main
Timothy Garton Ash, Oxford
Dr. Tessen von Heydebreck, Frankfurt am Main
Prof. Dr. Barbara Ischinger, Berlin
Dr. Josef Joffe, Hamburg
Prof. Dr. Hubert Markl, Munich
GMD Ingo Metzmacher, Hamburg
Dr. Jörg Mittelsten Scheid, Wuppertal
Prof. Dr. Harald Müller, Frankfurt am Main
Rabbi Julia Neuberger, London
Prof. Dr. Hans-Jürgen Quadbeck-Seeger, Ludwigshafen
Prof. Dr. Hans-Joachim Queisser, Stuttgart
Prof. Dr. Manfred Riedel, Halle
Prof. Dr. Rupert Scholz, Berlin
Prof. Dr. Christoph Schwöbel, Heidelberg
Daniel Vernet, Paris
Prof. Dr. Dr. Hartmut Weule, Karlsruhe

Managing Directors

Dr. Walter Homolka (Spokesman), Frankfurt am Main
Hanns Michael Hölz, Frankfurt am Main
Prof. Dr. Norbert Walter, Frankfurt am Main

Alfred Herrhausen Society
for International Dialogue

A DEUTSCHE BANK FORUM